John H. Battersby

Poems Patriotic

John H. Battersby

Poems Patriotic

ISBN/EAN: 9783337307103

Printed in Europe, USA, Canada, Australia, Japan

Cover: Foto ©Thomas Meinert / pixelio.de

More available books at **www.hansebooks.com**

POEMS

PATRIOTIC

BY

J. H. BATTERSBY

Not by might, nor by power, but by my Spirit, saith the Lord of hosts.—Zech. iv: 6.

NEW YORK
JULIUS R. HUTH
372 PEARL STREET
1894

TO

ALFRED W. DENNETT,

PHILANTHROPIST,

FRIEND OF MISSIONS,

THIS VOLUME IS RESPECTFULLY

INSCRIBED

BY THE AUTHOR.

CONTENTS.

	Page
AMERICA.	
Christopher Columbus	11
Our Predecessors	21
Freedom's Birth	23
Columbia	25
Our Wealth	26
Wooed and Wed	29
WASHINGTON—LINCOLN—GRANT.	
Our Washington	35
Lincoln	38
Death of General Grant	49
Tomb of General Grant	51
LOYALTY.	
The True Soldier	55
"'Bout Face!"	58
Virtue and Safety, One	60
The Soldier's Burial	63
JUSTICE.	
Hall of Justice	69
There is War	78
IN EUROPE.	
Empress Victoria	85
Germany	88
THE VITAL CONFLICT.	
The Victory of Truth	93

PREFACE.

POESY is a quill fallen from the pinion of an Archangel, as he flew by the earth on a mission of mercy. He who beholds it is charmed; he who wields it, all-glorious within.

It is an inspiration from above, the source of all beauty, joy, truth. The jewels of God's throne light the earth brighter than the noonday. Happy he with eyes open, to behold their radiance.

Political Economy, Liberty, Peace, are themes dear to the wise. In the lines following are painted, in plain colors, some of the beatitudes of Truth, and its victory, Freedom. The effort, tho' far below the lofty Ideal, may still, we trust, give the kind reader pleasing thoughts concerning its grandeur, and end. Praying that this may be so, and that God in all may be glorified;

I am

Yours in the Truth,

J. H. BATTERSBY.

America.

Christopher Columbus.

AND can it be, that human nature vile
Bound fast in chains, condemned to penury,
One who had come to be the great discoverer
Of this vast hemisphere in days of yore?
Yea, thus with mankind will it ever be,
The Blesser in the blessing is forgot.

As European nations traveled on
In search of conquest toward the western isles,
Ever alert, the mind of man began
To meditate upon the bright unknown.
Thus finite wisdom sought the infinite;
Read from creation's book whose pages glow
To bless this world of darkness with true light.

In course of time, became the theme sublime
Subject of much debate among the learned.
The old idea, that the world was flat,
Held on the shoulders of an Atlas broad,

Chased by a more enlightened age, fled like
A phantom on the verge of moral night.

The fact that Earth a spheroid might have been,
Thro' all the ages long, philosophic—
Deductions in the speculative mind
Of Eastern tho't, lit, as a flash of light,
Men's hearts athwart the path of that blest age.

In its fruition, came the fullness of
The time when Providence a leader gave.
Incarnate lived the truth in human soul,
When to Columbus came the holy call
Of God, to lead the nations farther on.

From infancy this theme his mind imbued,
Tho' gently his instructor led him forth
Into the clear convictions of his lot,
As manhood's strength assumed its ready aid.
In youth, it was an eaglet perched upon
His shoulders, e'er his footsteps to attend.
But, soon his fledged companion bore aloof
The bright ambition which he strove to gain.

Its piercing cry his beacon came to be,
Until, again, he clasped it in his breast.

A conflict with the forces of his state
Bro't forth and drilled the tenor of his mind,
As comes to be the lot of genius oft,
To struggle with adversity's keen edge.
Thus poverty assailed his rising hope.

To whom should he now turn, to ask for aid?
Not to the Hierarchal Powers, who scoffed
His plea, deemed so heretical, but to
Another chosen vessel of the Lord,
Who should th' oppressed of ev'ry land set free;
Should find asylum for God's holy ones.

Bro't before kings to prove his reasonings,
Some laughed, while others chided such a scheme.
Still, few there were—enough—to hear, believe.

As arguing with logic, all his own,
Before the Court of Spain, new zeal inspired
Him as he pleaded there, for armament
And men, to aid him in his hope forlorn.

The King and Queen were melted unto tears,
To think of what the future might disclose!
But where the legacy, from whence to draw
Sufficient sum, to furnish the demands
Of undertaking so immense?
       Woman,
Who led the race to ruin, oft hath led
It back toward its Eden, and its God.
Queen Isabella, moved by tho't so grand,
Plucked off her jewels! gave them for the hire
Of voyagers, to plow the sullen deep
In quest of empire.
      Caviled much the priests,
At act so ludicrous to unbelief.

The fair one, decked with more than earthly grace,
Persisted in her purpose to adorn
Her crown in garlands bright of wisdom rare.
And, thus embarked, the voyage soon began.

A course was taken west to reach the shore
Of India, so distant to the East.
Courage ran wild as they assayed the main,
Cheered by the throng that hail them from the shore.

For they knew not the trial of their faith,
As dreams of pleasure flitted thro' their minds.

Their gallant Captain bade the Court adieu—
Seized the command, to seek an unknown shore.
The seamen's song, the spreading of the sail,
The rolling wave, the grapple at the helm,
The genial skies, bespeak the longed-for smile
Of Providence to send them on their way.

The fleet of three, by the auspicious breeze,
Was wafted far beyond the bound of trade,
As days and weeks rolled lazily away.

And while they journeyed on, as yet, they had
Not seen the evidence of things beyond;
But, contrary, each earthly sign fell off.
The sea-weed, land birds, so accustomed to,
They left behind, facing a watery waste.
And, then, a bound was fixed to human hope.
Still,
    "Onward!"
        Came the cry from the Command.

Here, in these times, which test the faith of men,
We see the might of Truth again revealed.
The sailors, tired of watching, plan revolt.
Their bouyant hopes had plunged unto despair!
While all within them cried for distant home.

And who can tell the conflict of that mind
Left to its fears, its truths, its God, alone!
Of ev'ry phase of sympathy bereft,
But of that One, 'mid scenes of pain like these,
Calling upon his followers to prove;—
What, could ye not watch with me one brief hour!

Yea, what the fancies of that fateful tryst,
The tossings, conflict of the struggling soul.
Deeper to him than ocean's deepest grave—
Dashing above the cycles of the stars,
The tho't of God! in his immensity.
From out whose mighty grasp he cannot leap;
Beyond whose bound he, fearing, may not pass;
Nor can withdraw himself from his blest will,
Without a suicidal wresting from all good.

Lo, while from man and earth he seems aloof,
An Angel's wings around him gather in,
As came the draught of comfort to his lips,
Which strengthened him to stand erect, unmoved.

Thus he, the hero of the hour, is firm.
With hope his anchor, grace became his stay;
Fear held him firm unto conviction's helm—
The fear of God, under whose wide control
He yielded to be led unto the end.

The raging deep tost to and fro the ships,
Yet were they never separated: till
The cry of
   "Land, ho!"
      rang along the deck—
Along the fleet.
Every eye and ear,
And muscle, strain to catch a glimpse of forms
Faint, indistinct, still rising to their view.—
"Land, ho!"
   the sailors echo in return,
As to the topmasts each in haste ascends.

Now are the tips of dreamy distant hills
Seen from afar.
                They shout for joy! they dance!—
The ships glide on.
                Yet he, who in the hour
Of disaffection spurned them not, is now
The centre of their beatific joy.
They kneel, they grasp him by the feet! they kiss
His hands! and tell him how, while some did doubt,
They e'er believed his prophesy as true.
While those belligerent, thirsting for blood—
His blood—skulked off in fear, waiting his eye.

Now, as they near the verdant shore, an age
Of wonder 'trances every mind! And there
Shall wonder greet them, in the savage gaze
Of God's brown sons, who sight them from the shore.

Behold them land! with cross uplifted high,
According to the custom of those days.
Devoutly kneeling, see Columbus bow:
Taking the land for King Immanuel.
The flag of state by them is then unfurled.

Bringing choice specimens of western wealth,
We see him spreading sail for home again.
Then what a scene of blest festivity
Brightens the court of Ferdinand of Spain!
And how the honors of that brilliant hour
Reflected credit to the beauteous Queen,
Whose wisdom shone above those jewels bright
Which she renounced, to covet things more rare.

The world, astounded at the joyous news—
Smitten with grief at former unbelief—
Made ready to take part in this delight;
Sending embassadors, as homage due
To holy greatness in Columbus' faith
And true fidelity, till fame was won
Above all navigators; while to man,
Oppressed and murdered by his fellow-man,
A blest asylum opened, free from fear.

Painful as was this trial of his faith—
Yet fraught with consciousness of duty done—
The cup he drank, placed to all human lips
Who have, by faith, the mighty conflict won
Of life's bright calling, even that of woe!

Lest, being overcome of much success,
He might the glory take unto himself,
And dream of his own wisdom as the source
Of his renown.
           Hence, on his third return
From western lands, they put him into bonds;
Yea, on the plaint of traitor, held in chains
Those useful hands which wrought such wondrous weal;
Yea, still more, let him die neglected, poor!
Thus do the blind oft slay their useful men;
Then, afterward, garnish their tombs with gold.

Yet, glory never-fading crowns his brow.
Rejoicing, he beholds the triumph now,
And its rich harvest to the end of time,
Even for aye, unto the praise of God.
                              Amen.

Nov. 1892.

Our Predecessors.

There was a race of dusky skin,
Whose weal the Lord delighted in;
Who hunted o'er these Forest Lands,
Who fished upon these Lakes and Strands.

But they the truth of God forgot.
They worshiped, yet, they knew not what.
War paint was found within their tent;
The poisoned dart its fury lent;
Till many bright and lovely spots
Became the haunts of bloody plots,
Whose vengeance slacked its thirst in blood—
A sickening scene—a dismal flood!
Blind superstition rent his mind
Who feared the mystic voice behind.

The fullness of the time drew nigh,
When Justice, looking from on high,
Beheld the flowing of their cup—
Decreed that they should drink it up.
And when their dark sins balanced o'er,

His fury He did on them pour!
Warning to nations, far and near,
Who fail to make the Lord their fear.

Upon their once polluted ground,
A People owning God is found.
Their banners float upon the breeze;
Their songs of praise among the trees,
In camps, on mounts and on the shore,
Proclaim that darkness is no more.
For superstition's lurid dread
Has to the bats and vampires fled,
Before the rising of the sun
Whose cycles thro' the ages run;
Whose rays dispense the priceless boon —
Hailing with joy the brilliant noon —
Of knowledge, virtue, ev'ry grace
Essential to the human race.

Freedom's Birth.

God has revealed unto his creature, man,
His providence of grace, his Gospel Plan.
Its wealthy messages to us unfurled,
Proclaim His love unto a fallen world.
This plan disclosed, the salient truth is taught
That, greatest blessings oft, at birth, are fraught
With greatest struggles. Clearly this is shown
In God's redemption of His loved, His own.

And so, as to Europia once clung
The fangs of bigotry. When Conscience, stung
To anguish by truths unrelenting goad,
Labored to free herself from her great load.
Amid her throes of fearful agony,
Looking in vain for peace, or liberty,
A haven for the sore-oppressed is found,
Amid these western wilds a hallowed ground
For Virtue's shrine; where conscience, eased of pain,
Shall find relief from errors grievous chain.

A Prophet see! in holy reverence bow
To place the laurel on fair Freedom's brow,
Where bigotry shall loose its wonted sway;
Here Freedom's Song becomes the nation's lay.

And thus Columbia arose to view!
Her emblem bright, the Stars, and Stripes, and Blue.

Precious the Freight within the Mayflower strong,
Which sighed and prayed thro' all the voyage long
Of the Atlantic: and, when on the shore,
Kneeled there to praise God! who had bro't them o'er.

Before their eyes His wonders were displayed.
On Plymouth Rock the bulwarks strong were laid
Of God's great reign of peace. O, Nation blest!
Coming from o'er the sea to find thy rest—
Rest from the proud Oppressor's galling yoke.
For, now, the gloomy spell is ever broke
Which reeked disaster on the humble Band
Who sought and found new empire in this land,
Where liberty of conscience is allowed;
Where equity is meeted to the Proud.

Columbia.

Thou great Columbia! broad and grand!
Bright is thy clear and pearly Strand;
Many thy Mountains vast and high,
Towering upward toward the sky;
Broad thy long Rivers, deep their bed;
Wealthy thy Mines of Iron and Lead;
Rich are thy fields of purest Gold;
Treasures of Coal and Wood untold.
Choicest of all the lands of earth,
The home of Virtue's sterling worth.
Fair are thy Summers; bright thy Stars;
Valiant the victories of thy Wars.
Blessed the Shrine of Democracy—
Throne of God's priceless Liberty!

Our Wealth.

Many the Tribes and Clans which roam
From far, to seek in thee a home.
The strange Mongolian finds estate
Within thy walls, O Golden Gate!
The Ethiopian, dusky skin,
Thy warm Savannas glories in:
The sturdy Briton plows the main
To bear abroad thy Gold and Grain;
And, European Nations hear
Thy praises sounding far and near.

How ripe the culture of thy schools—
The mart of scientific rules—
Thy Universities and Halls
Of learning which the student calls
Philosophique, where ever dwell
Sages of lore, whose magic spell
Wooes youthful minds to love the light,
To hate the wrong, to choose the right.

Inventive genius springs from this—
The handmaid of domestic bliss.
The Railway, Telegraph and 'Phone
Marry the States. While all alone
The mourners sit around the fire,
A message leaps along the wire.
Electric harmony thrills o'er
The hemisphere, from shore to shore.

And, so, fair Justice has her sway—
The font of Truth's ethereal day.
Her lofty domes, her minarets
The culprit ne'er, thro' fear, forgets;
But flees beyond the nation's bound,
Like wild game chased by horse and hound,
Far to the rebel's dark retreat:
For here he finds no mercy-seat!

Here may the widow find a shelter,
When sorrows o'er the homestead pelter.
Before the tender Infant's wail,
The Autocrat is doomed to fail.

Real Spartan courage guards the graves
Of those who are true Freedom's Braves.
Thy fortresses and strong ramparts
Are laid in valiant human hearts,
Whose loyalty like shot is hurled
Against the treason of the world.

Thou lookst not for earthly crown,
To be the staff of thy renown.
The grace which builds fair Virtue's throne,
Makes each pure heart a living stone.

Wooed and Wed.

BEHOLD! fair Liberty is wed
To honest Virtue. And, 'tis said,
    They dwell in peace together.
Proud License tho't to woo the Maid,
But, when his plans were duly laid,
    He found she was too clever.

Then, Croesus fancied he could win
The one whom rich men glory in:
    His gems and brilliant rubies
Were judged to be of worth enough
To stay the course of her rebuff,
    And deck her crown with beauties!

Thus Pleasure, donned with nobby air,
Desired to gain the maiden fair
    By one device, or other;
And so, he to her cottage went,
His every charm its power lent,
    To play the part of lover.

While Honor, with his kingly crown,
Believed the flame of his renown
    Would meet her approbation.
Yea, courtly pomp would seal his bliss—
Would gain for him the gentle Miss,
    And elevate her station.

Ambition, too, with pleasing talk,
Came tripping up the garden walk
    To her benign seclusion.
At first he cried, What do I care!
Then came the vacant foolish stare,
    Which witnessed his delusion.

"But how," you ask, "did Virtue gain
The bridal race; and then, attain
    To all its joy and glory;
Leaving the others in the lurch,
As laggards trimmed with rod of birch?"
    Well, listen to my story:—

The Maiden's keen ability
Saw that, without integrity,
    The married state could never—
While Gold is strong, and Honor high,

Or License dare the Laws defy—
  Bind wedded ones forever.

Tho' Pleasure may attract the sense,
And Trickery his arts dispense,
  To satisfy the erring;
Yet, Principle must needs control
The warm desire of Freedom's soul,
  And consecrate the wedding.

'Tis Purity! the bond that holds.
Domestic bliss such love unfolds;
  And so, too, of a nation.
Truth builds her own safe citadel,
Defending all her forces well;
  Nor dreams of hesitation.

Yea, Virtue builds republics strong.
Deception weakens all along
  The line of their embankments.
So, fair Columbia, be wise!
The fortress Truth do not despise;
  Nor leer at her enchantments.

Unfurl thy banners to the breeze!
Till every jealous nation sees
    Fond Liberty's espousal
To constant Virtue, true and grand!
Whose wedlock hath redeemed our land
    From slavery's carousal.

But, who the author of this grace
Which calms our troubled populace,
    Confirming every blessing?
'Tis God!—'tis God! at whose great throne
The Plymouth Fathers bowed alone;
    In Him all good possessing.

He framed our great Republic's plan;
Equality ordained for man.
    This wisdom God hath given,
Can foil the luckless Tyrant's snare,
Can all his motley forces dare,
    Till slavery be riven.

Washington.

Lincoln.

Grant.

Our Washington.

A LITTLE boy in terror stood!
    His parent coming nigh:—
"My Son, why did you cut that wood?"
    He said, "I cannot lie!

"O Father, I have felled that tree,
    Destroyed each leafy bow;
But, as you taught me true to be,
    Will not deny it now!"

The father's heart was pleased to claim
    Truth's honor for his son,
And hence the fame of the great name
    Of our GEORGE WASHINGTON!

If truth could be, in early years,
    His confidence and joy,
May it not quench the sullen fears
    Of every girl and boy?

If, by a father's wise command,
    Obedient love be won,
May not the children of our land
    Be brave as WASHINGTON!

And who can tell how many youths,
    By his example taught,
Have chosen for defence pure Truth's
    Bright blade, and with it fought.

He bore the most important test,
    That, Truth can make one great!
Can lead a man to choose the best
    In interests of state.

For it becomes the Cornerstone
    Of all true government.
Founded upon its base alone,
    The people are content.

When confidence is thus built up
    In man's own brotherhood,
Then may our nation drink the cup
    Of ev'ry social good.

Then can we boldly measure arms
    With other human races;
And on our banners gild the charms
    Of Virtue's mighty graces.

When War is fully overthrown;
    When cease the cannon's rattle;
Shall have acquired Truth his own,
    Have won his final battle,

Peace, righteousness and joy shall rest
    Above man's vain opinion;
Edenic beauties manifest
    The strength of Christ's dominion.

Lincoln.

Behold a nation dark, from Afric's strand,
Flood bright savannas of Christopherland.
The rice and cotton fields, tilled by their brawn,
In wealth and beauty lay to greet the dawn.

Tho' poorly clad, toiling from day to day,
The welkin rang at eve with many a lay
Of touching melody, of fervent prayer,
To chase the phantoms dark of earthly care.
Wanting but little — asking even less —
Oft were they bro't thro' seasons of distress
To know the bound of human woe, and feel
Asperity's keen lash, without repeal.
For, lords usurped the freedom of their will —
Held them in chains of cruel bondage still.

Their youth, blithe lads, would stray from eve till noon,
To catch Opossum, tree the wild Raccoon;
Or welt the cabin floor in merry dance,

Beneath the silent moonbeam's silvery glance,
While Dinah thrummed the time on Tambourine,
Until the noon of night. Then were they seen
Wending their way unto the quiet fold
Which weariness called home.
                          The "Mammy" old
Affording nurse unto her infant lord,
Hummed o'er her lullaby in sweet accord;
Stirred up the hoe-cake; spread the frugal board—
Could more than this such penury afford?
Adorned her humble hearth, ere called at morn,
In snow white apron—to the manor born—
Where spacious halls, verandas broad and long,
Gave air of comfort to the idle throng
Who daily met to praise the god of ease
And wine, choice, sparkling from the purple lees.

Yet were there seen examples bright and clear,
Tho' rare, of masters who had learned to fear
The Lord and knew the power of his might,
That He forever standeth for the right
Of enslaved. The old, the youth, the weak,
In grateful memory their praises speak,
Who gave unto the hungry of their store,

Who never drove the needy from their door.
And many tears were shed upon the grave
Of "good ole Massy," guardian of the slave.

And others still, wrought on by grace divine,
Received those truths which make the just to shine.
The Golden Rule to them became a law,
Who in it good for all men clearly saw.
Thus manumission came to be their choice,
Who listened to the call of Wisdom's voice.

Still, many were oppressed with fear of wrong,
Tortured with pain; sleepless the whole night long.
From off the block, like cattle, were they sold,
To glut the rancor of corroding gold.
The dearest social ties asunder rent.
Mid scenes of mourning were their moments spent.
Father and son, aye, son with sister dear,
Clasped each in arms, with words of sorrow drear.
Mother from nursling, torn away from breast,
Sought long in vain for sympathy, or rest.

The keen lash welts had cut upon their backs,
Leaving for life their hellish tempest-tracks.

All social interests, all right to know,
All feelings planted in the heart to grow,
Were them debarred who even hated life!
Which came to be to them one scene of strife.

But he who heard the cry of Israel,
Who understood their pain and sorrow well
In bondage, stood up to defend their cause,
To abrogate the proud usurper's laws.
He answered prayer for their down-trodden race;
Proffered the power of his saving grace.
The cup of their affliction flowing o'er,
God spake, in tones which pierced th' oppressor sore,
Saying,
    It is enough! The right I claim
To vindicate my just and holy name.
I will repay, will restoration make;
Will scourge the guilty, for my great name's sake.
For the oppressed shall blood drip from my rod,
To let the nations know that I am God.
My people I will not in bondage leave,
For they by faith unto my promise cleave.—

Come from the north, O noble men and brave.
Ye warriors, gird on the sword, to save.
Mount! plunge the spur! wield ye the battle-ax!
Haste to the conflict. Let not might relax!
A million horse, fleet as the wind, shall sweep
Over thy pleasant land; thy vintage reap.
Cut down thy sons and fathers in their might,
O thou ursurper of all human right!
Scatter the aged, feeble from their birth;
Mow down thy fields of corn; enfire the earth
And forests; plague thee with a longing plea.
Then shalt thou let my people go forth free.

From gath'ring clouds, the lurid darts of light
In skies political, at length shone bright.
For sin—a nation's sin—strove for the ground,
To far extend its territorial bound.

Astutest statesmen failed to see the scope
Of its intent, until the sudden hope
For open conflict on the battle-field;
Where Wrong, or Right, must to the struggle yield.

The northern mountains trembled with the dread.
Shore lashed the mighty seas to wake the dead.
The lofty cedars bowed their heads in prayer,
As upward belched contention everywhere.

Then came the call to arms—the clash of steel.
Drunken with carnage, mighty forces reel!
In fearful courage did the armies kill.
Foe against foe, they slaughtered with a will!
In expectation of the nation's fall,
Darkness had veiled the scene in horror's pall!

Blood stained the rivers in their onward flow,
The thirsty soil sated its greed for woe:
The air rent with the din, the groan of war.
Hear ye the battle-cry, sounding afar.

The beauteous Hudson ran her forces down;
Penobscot's saber glistened with renown;
The Mississippi drank the crimson stain,
While bold Ohio wrestled on her main.

Manassas felt the thunder of their shock,
Where cannon roared, and battered musket stock;

Corinth and Shiloh drank their tale of woes,
As Grant and Rosecrans struck telling blows.
On Lookout Mountain rose the star of hope,
As fell in war the great, misguided Pope.
Valor exulted Independence Day,
As Vicksburg rose—to fall! in blank dismay.
Sherman's triumphal march to compass Lee,
Swept down upon Atlanta and the sea.
The stalward band rose o'er the dismal flood,
While Gettysburg baptized the land in blood;—
The Wilderness! where shot and terror fell,
And fire arose from out the womb of hell.
Then came the chase of conflict, spear to heel,
Until, reluctant, came the sore appeal;
The laying down of arms; paroled release.
The struggle o'er, embattled tempests cease!

The Queen of Bourbon sat in regal state,
Musing upon the sadness of her fate.
Her broken vows alone had made her queen.
In sackcloth dark her courtiers all were seen.
And as she plied the magic of her hand,
To emphasize with force her stern command,

Her face, unveiled, disclosed a flood of tears
Which, dashing oft, gave token of her fears.—

"Haste to the marts of Albion away—
Haste to the Seine, where balmy zephyrs play—
Haste to the nations drunken with our wine.
Call aid for aid, around Nimbulo's* shrine.
Come, ye exalted Powers of the earth,
Behold your daughter travailing in birth!
Hie thee, stand by the pillars of my throne:
Fight as the brave or, forfeit life thine own!
Stay by, until I rend the Starry Flag.
The "Stars and Bars" its folds in blood shall drag!
From this dire war, a Nation fair shall rise,
Whose praises shall ascend to kiss the skies.

Then God from heaven looked upon the world,
And saw the new-made graves; the vengeance hurled;
The flashing energy of soul 'gainst soul;
The widow's tears, the tide of anguish roll.
He answered not the prayers of fetish sires,
Whose angered passions blazed from altar fires;

* Genius of Slavery.

But, chose the feeble cry of the oppressed,
To whom he came, in time to give them rest.
The Union Banners were by him upheld,
Who all their foes, in all their malice, quelled.

The doom of kingdoms sometimes is involved
    Upon the point of sabre or, of pen.
And, what the sword could not alone have solved,
    The pen of LINCOLN executed then!

A bandage for earth's woes was woven there,
To staunch the flow of death and mad despair.
Behold a Nation rising from the tomb
Of wretchedness, divested of its gloom;
Mocking the chains which bound it to the dead—
Leaving their graves, like Christ, their living head.

Sing to the world, ye bards, of joys sublime,
Of victory along the path of time.
The mighty shout rises along the line
Of battle, where the glittering bayonets shine.
Wrong to the Right, by force is made to yield.
Cheer! for the right hath won the bloody field.

The vanquished hosts in fear and trouble fall,
Their subtle purpose driven to the wall.
While consternation ev'ry bosom fills,
They haste to reach the covert of the hills.
Hemmed in, they falter, yield the strife, give o'er—
Promise to raise the rebel flag no more.

Thus shackles from a nation's rights were broke.
Enfranchised citizens their claims bespoke,
To wield the power of a freeman's hand—
In phalanx for the true and right to stand;
Showing the world their rising chivalry
To guard the land of their nativity;
To stand, true statesmen, 'neath the starry flag,
Nor let its colors in dishonor drag;
To war, if need be, for their natal sod;
Noble and brave, as are the sons of God.

Enwrapped in garments stained with gore his own,
Having in wisdom filled a monarch's throne,
The haughty Chieftain, drawing near the close,
Serene, secure and blest, entered repose
Covered with glory! Here we carve his name
High in the architraves of worthy fame.

Let no unhallowed footsteps here intrude,
To desecrate a nation's gratitude.
Here never may the hand of treason mar—
Never again such woe the nation jar.
From hence a light unto the nations shines,
To show them all kind Providence designs
That, man no more his fellow man may wrong;
That Liberty shall be earth's triumph song.
Emblazonry of truth shall never rust.
Embalmed in memory e'er live the just.

Death of General Grant.

Angel's wings are hovering now,
    Over grand McGregor;
Quiet soothes the Conqueror's brow,
    Bathed in peaceful slumber;
Fragrant odors fill the place—
    Faithful prayers ascending—
By a Nation pleading grace,
    Low in silence bending.

Tho' the heavens be opprest
    By the people's mourning,
Yet the glowing of the west
    Shines with hope's adorning;
For the faithful heraldry
    Of a bright to-morrow —
Fruit of hard-fought victory—
    Shall disperse all sorrow.

Now the shining Angel Band
    Come a little nearer;
While they bear, to their own land,
    Him who lives forever
In the hearts of all the good,
    And in yon bright Heaven;
Who for Freedom nobly stood,
    Till her foes were driven.

Tomb of General Grant.

OTHER proud captains, noble men and true,
    Fought hard and well to occupy this throne
In human hearts and human destiny,
    But thou, great Chieftain, dost ascend alone.

The sordid chains of traffic in the blood
    Of the meek African, sorely enslaved,
Were by thy skill asunder cleft in war;
    A nation, by thy valor, hast thou saved.

The fields where thou hast shown thy heraldry
    Of Freedom's cause, are over grown with peace:
High Heaven calls to arms thy troops no more;
    Strife's battle-cry, its groans, its dying, cease.

Here rest! until the waking of that morn
    When heavenly hosts, having attained renown,
Shall hail thee, Conqueror! to that blest land
    Where laurels, never fading, deck thy crown.

1892.

Loyalty.

The True Soldier.

Deep conviction stirred the Soldier,
    In our bloody Civil War,
When the "Battle Cry of Freedom"
    Woke the Nation, near and far.

Some were placid, some opposing,
    While they drew a soldier's pay;
Others gloried in adorning
    Their fair forms in colors gay.

Some delighted in the circus
    Of a brilliant Dress Parade:
But when flew the deadly missiles,
    All those men were sore afraid.

Now comes on the real soldier,
    Humble in his mien, but, true;
While amid the din of battle
    Never at a loss to do.

See his grim and pallid visage
    As he draws his trusty steel;
See the gleam on spear and helmet,
    At the clarion's appeal.

There, he falls! again, he rises!
    Still the battle to pursue.
Lo, his wounds with crimson streaming!
    Yet he keeps his rank in view.

What the purpose of his courage?
    Is he an adventurer?
What tho't nerves him for the conflict,
    Makes him more than conqueror?

'Tis the spirit that is in him.
    For a Principle he fights.
He the guardian of the Homestead,
    In whose safety he delights.

He is fighting for the freedom
    Of the long degraded Slave,
To deliver him from thraldom;
    And, his Native Land to save.

In his step the "swing of conquest,"
    He is striving for the right.
Hence his valor in the battle,
    Hence his mighty strength to fight.

Finally, his efforts triumph.
    Wrong must yield to Virtue's pow'r.
Thus the great Vanguard of Freedom
    Conquered, in the trying hour.

"'Bout Face!"

A MAN may take command
    Before he knows the drill.—
The memory of Bull Run flight
    Is with the Nation still.

To learn the tame details,
    A man must rise from naught—
Must know the "ins and outs" of things,
    And be in patience taught.

The iron bands of War
    Were welded in the fight
By deadly Conquest's mighty arm,
    Trained to uphold the right.

Recruits in dress parade
    Oft flourish and are gay,
Who, in the thickest of the strife,
    Escape another way.

Are taught, on land and sea,
    The sons of royal birth,
Those rudiments by which they hope
    To gain the realms of earth.

Just Providence decrees
    That Veterans shall gain
The brightest laurels of redress,
    Where laggards seek in vain.

Virtue and Safety, One.

In early times, when Rome was young,
    And brave, and pure, and grand;
When nobles wise in majesty
    Ruled o'er the mighty land;
Before the Star of Bethlehem
    Had risen on the world,
And reason was the only light
    Which all their tho't unfurled;
They then were made the arbiters
    Of all the nations round.
While daily, at their cities' gates,
    Ambassadors were found.

They were the chosen umpires of
    Political debates;
To freedom rescued thrall; defined
    The boundaries of states;

Till, thus did she become, at last,
  The savior of her race.
The brightest glory statesmen wear,
  Her annals proudly grace.

The time, however, came when she,
  Proud of her sons no longer,
Yielded herself to wear the yoke
  Of nations wiser, stronger.
Whence the occasion of this fall,
  From honor high made humble?
Did they thus clamber up so far,
  To take the greater tumble!

No—They were tempted, first of all,
  To covet throne and pow'r
Where they were called to arbitrate;
  Then came the fatal hour!
Where confidence was once bestowed,
  There entered keen suspicion.
Then gathered round a raging flood
  Which chastened their ambition.

Their principles, and not their name,
    Were what the nations trusted:
Hence the occasion of their fame,
    Before for gain they lusted.

Thus shall we find, in this our age,
    The excellence of candor,
To guide the patriot and sage
    Far from the shoals of rancor.

MORAL.

When statesmen would aspire so high,
    Would dictate to the nations,
Their own blest country's only weal
    Is VIRTUE'S firm foundations.

The Soldier's Burial.

Out by the copse on the sandy hill,
Near the meandering mountain rill,
There have they laid him, cold and still;
    The valiant Volunteer.

Oft had he met with the mirthful "boys;"
There had he shared with them in their joys;
Hence the deep grief their tho't employs
    Around the silent bier.

Yearly they bivouacked in camp, of yore.
But he shall march with them never more,
As thro' the clover field they bore
    Their comrade's clay so dear.

He nobly stood with the faithful Band;
Bravely he struck, with a mighty hand,
To save the freedom of our land!
    A sturdy pioneer.

Seven are left to revere his name,
Rehearse the glory of his meek fame.
Yet, like the rebels he o'ercame,
    Death shall each member sear.

Solemn the voice of the sad refrain;
Sadly the mourners their tears restrain;
For he hath vanquished grief and pain,
    Crowning his bold career.

"Load!" cries the officer of the guard;
"Aim!" as if Death they would there bombard!
"Fire!" and the heavens quickly jarred
    Over the form austere.

Loudly the echo ran down the glen,
As deep emotion inspired the men—
"Load!" see them rally; now, again;
    Over the mound raised here.

There, o'er the grave, each has stacked his gun,
As roll the mists toward the setting sun;
For they have wrought all can be done,
    To laud their brave compeer.

Fair ones shall gather around his tomb,
Strewing rare flowers of brightest bloom,
Divesting death of all its gloom
    In sorrow's loving tear.

Reveille no more wakes at the morn,
Tho' uniform his remains adorn.
As there it lies beneath, forlorn,
    Angels his spirit cheer.

Justice.

Hall of Justice.

Far down town, 'mid scenes terrestrial,
    In the region of the "*World*,"
Where the "News Kings" rule industrial,
    And opinion is unfurled;
Where the buildings now are rising
    Which eclipse the Queen of light;
And two cities one comprising,
    There with bridal span unite;
Where the hazy clouds electric
    Form the girdle of the way—
Gotham's ready dialectic,
    Flashing Fact and Light as day;
Where the hosts of Scribblers flourish;
    Judges sit in solemn state;
Politicians freedom nourish,
    In sequestered lobbies wait;

Lo Justice sits, with folded hands,
    To listen to the Menial's prayer

Who, tho' restrained by legal bands,
    Expects to find protection there.

"Behold! Fair Justice!" loud he cries,
    "I come thine excellence to plead;
That thou wouldst cover my assize,
    Wouldst save the just, in time of need.

"I entered Croesus' stately Manse
    To prosecute my humble trade,
As by the moonbeams' gentle glance
    I saw what plunder could be made.
But, lo, the landlord forced me thence,
    Without the slightest warning given.
I raised my arm in self-defence—
    To his proud heart the knife was driven!
His friends, assembled here, agree
    That they are bound to see me die!
But, here I stand to make my plea.
    Must I be slain, while help is nigh?—

There bows a trembling one, alone,
    While weeds of mourning wreath her head;

The pallor of the grave her own.
    She sees the object of all dread,
The ruffian, clad in garb once worn
    By her beloved. Hides her face
Away from him whose clutch had torn
    Out from her hold his fond embrace,
And plunged the dagger to his heart!—
    By night, the phantom of her dream.
Nestled, her little Birds apart
    Are grouped, who fear the eagle's scream.

Her tale is told of that dire night;
    Portrayed the horrifying scene,
Of all her hopes on earth the blight;
    Identifies the robber's mien.
Those words are simple, brief, but true—
    Clear as the limpid waters flow;
Yet, like a dart their aim pursue,
    And terror strike, where'er they go.
For truth is mighty, and will tell;
    Its holy triumph we assume.
Many a rogue has heard its knell
    Proclaiming his approaching doom.—

Now, again, the culprit rises
  'Neath the great tribunal throne.
Tho' blest wisdom he despises,
  Still with Law he wrestles, prone.
Then he sends to haunts he frequents,
  Calls for aid his fickle "Pal;"
Seeks his bristling antecedents;
  Tries his "pull political:"
Scans the rigid face of Justice
  To behold one ray of light.
In the God of truth her trust is,
  Till be manifest the right.

After come the Legal Talent,
  While their witnesses confess;
Long conclusions climb the ascent,
  Judge and Jury sorely press.
All the loop-holes in the netting
  Of the Law are fully known;
While her steadfastness regretting,
  Vice must Virtue, first, dethrone.

Champions of right ne'er falter
  At the fierce forensic fire.

Their grand purpose to exalt her
    In whose might they never tire.

Argued ev'ry point in order,
    Laboring for life and weal,
Note the diligent Recorder,
    Hear the passionate appeal!

Maidens, with but little decence,
    Now appear to bear him flowers
Plucked in haste, with loving prepense,
    From the vine in Passion's Bowers.

As Cause by Cause is made to bow,
    An awful silence reigns around;—
The veil is flung from Justice' brow!
    Her golden words as music sound;—

"The Balances of Truth were laid
    Before the earth's foundations.
In them their Maker oft hath weighed
    The chiefs of many nations.
'Twas by their quick, unerring trend
    Belteshazzar was found wanting.

Yea, many noble judges bend
    Before this bar, recanting.
Yet, wise the people who are just,
    This standard choose for action;
Whose firm decisions show their trust
    In Truth, without retraction.

"The Principles of Government
    Were once by God appointed.
Founded thereon, our Laws resent
    All argument disjointed.
The Facts upon their merits stand,
    As judged by truth's conclusion,
Tho' it should bring, throughout the land,
    The Wayward to confusion.

"While here, before me, kneels to-day
    One whom the Furies wanted,
Whom their intrigues have led astray,
    To take a life undaunted;
The case is proven beyond doubt.
    This terror, horrifying,

Brings ill to all the good about.
    The Innocent are dying!

"Thy Counsel sues for clemency.
    Lo, it shall here be given
To Fatherless in misery,
    Like Lambs by Panthers driven!
The consequences of thy course
    Begin their sad requitals;
And, now, the Laws unyielding force
    Requires thy trembling vitals!
There, on the innocent, thy hand
    Was laid in cruel malice.
So shall my word, at once, demand
    Thou drink the Murderer's Chalice!
Blood calls for blood! Thy brother's voice
    Crieth to God for vengeance.
Let all who love His name rejoice;
    Who place on Him dependence.

"The Executioner shall hail
    Thee to Electric Chamber—

Shall make thy mournful mother wail!
    To rid the earth of danger.

"Go, vilest reptile, to thy doom!
    Go, pray for one brief season.
Enter the portals of thy tomb
    To pay the price of treason.

"Perchance, a just and angry God
    May see in thee repentance.
From out the virtue of his rod
    Find there his mercy's entrance."

The writhing culprit back recoils
    Far from the throne immortal!
He sees how useless all his toils
    To gain its lofty portal.

The terror-stricken Widowed Heart
    Goes forth in meek contentment;
While all the Good, the Wise, depart
    Honoring Truth's resentment.

In dens of dark despair behold
  The vicious grimly cower,
Hissing their curses manifold,
  Yet—fear the Ruling Power!

MORAL.

Blessed Municipality,
  Where Justice deals with prudence;
Where Law observes equality:
  Where Crime has no indulgence.

How vile the terror and the curse,
  Where Law succumbs to Plunder.
When Rapine shall the laws disperse,
  We make the greatest blunder.

1889.

There is War!

Mother Earth rides serenely thro' heavenly space,
    While yet, on her breast is commotion.
Aye, the battle of elements, which oft deface
    A deal on the land and the ocean.

There is storm when the thunder-bolt cleaves the
    hot air,
    Of death plows the deep gastly furrow;
When the terrific gleam frights the beast in his lair,
    As the fair lady faints in the borough.

And sublime is the tempest which rules o'er the sea,
    That mounts on the crest of the billow,
Plunging deep in the caverns where vast treasures be;
    Yet, tossing the ship on its pillow.

There is also fierce strife in the midst of the world,
    The city and nation disturbing;

Where vile missiles of wrath in dark vengeance are hurled
    By men who the laws are subverting.

There is war on the continent—war on the fleet;
    While foes international bristle
Quite closely upon the black heels of retreat,
    To capture—?—the down of a thistle!

But, contentions there are in the Church and the State—
    Sometimes betwixt one and the other—
Where are fightings with swords or, with pens, in debate,
    Which sever the title of brother.

Also, wars intellectual. Science declares
    About pre-adamic delusion;
Tries to bring that dear Bible of ours into snares,
    And those who believe, to confusion.

Hard and long may the rat gnaw with vim on the file,
    Its might of incision to master;

For the toothless old gums, when rewarded erewhile,
    Shall bleed forth their woeful disaster.

There is war in the Tropics, and war at the Poles,
    Electric equation producing:
"Probabilities" never their fury controls,
    Tho' Science her lore is diffusing.

There is war in the stylish arena of wealth,
    Lest Great should appear to be Greatest!
Also war about Medicine, or Laws of Health;
    Or, how we should dress "in the latest."

There is war in the Newspaper Editor's brain
    About that edition on Sunday;
On the slate of his profits he foots a fair gain,
    But, finds a deficit on Monday.

In the church of the Little Papa there is war,
    In this blessed country of learning,
Lest the Free Schools should knock out the light of his star—
    Should bring to remembrance his yearning.

Some there will ever be who stand silent, aghast!
　　To see the advancement of knowledge;
And who fight with hot hate in their hearts, to the last,
　　The Primary School and the College.

There is strife in a branch of the Puritan Church
　　Because of their "blue orthodoxy:"
Where pure Scriptural Truth leaves the wrong in the lurch,
　　And shows Calvin's heterodoxy.

So we hear of debate in the Wesleyan fold—
　　That church of historic revival!
For proud lovers of pleasure and lovers of gold
　　Are striving to cherish her rival.

There is war in the minds of the people at large,
　　To know if dire Electrocution
Is so sweet as to cradle the Murderer's charge,
　　Whose Victim demands execution.

The various commotions of nature may jar;
　　They only annoy our deficience.

The great moral conflicts of man really mar!
   They bring on remorse with persistence.

There is war! There is war! As the conflict we view,
   Each soldier is girt for the battle:
But the conquest is gained by the earnest and true,
   Who fear not the loud cannon's rattle.

All forms of delusion and error shall fall.
   Our God, from above send the power!
Give the love of thy truth and thy fear unto all:
   Then, wars and dissentions are over.

1890.

In Europe.

Empress Victoria.

HAIL! gentle Spring! fair blossom of the year.
Hail! happy Queen! to us devoutly dear.
Rejoicing in thy long and peaceful reign,
Thy people greet thee! o'er thy vast domain.

As vernal beams bring joy to all the earth,
So, peace and gladness sprang forth at thy birth,
Whose early days were draped in virtue's robe—
Sound of whose wisdom sped around the globe.

Fifty and two, the years that thy renown,
In purity so bright, hath decked a crown—
Nineteen when thou, a virgin frail, yet fair,
Received thy diadem, with graces rare
Among the sovereigns of that drear time,
When kings were but the heraldry of crime.

As on thy brow lit England's coronet,
The Source of glory thou didst not forget;

Nor veer across thy Courts tempestuous sea,
Whate'er of good, or ill, it bro't to thee.

Well didst thou choose, as England's great Foreward,
The only true and ever living Lord!
Throughout the grandeur of her realm's extent
His Word became the Code of Government—
And, while the blood of wars her banners stained,
This confidence her victories have gained
That, triumph sits upon that stately Throne
Whose faith and hope are fixed on God alone!

Diffusion of this earth-renewing light
Hath been thy mission, thro' the moral night
Whose hazy wings have fled from off thy shores.
The Sun of gospel peace benignly soars.

Thy wars have bro't the Gospel in their wake,
Whose glorious truths the world in terror shake;
That, from all fear they may, believing, roam
To find in Christian State a happy home.
Thus have the Isles oft waited at thy gate;
Thus nations foreign of thy strength debate.

Wealth, Art and Science rule within thy realm,
As Peace sits cooing on its sturdy helm;
Which, from the rising to the setting sun,
Hath, with its circuit, equal journey run.

Hail! beauteous Queen! may thy *victorious* sway
Extend and be promoted, day by day;
Until the Earth, won by the King of Kings,
Be ushered into joys of better things.

1890.

Germany.

Bulwark of nations, far and near;
Your mighty dread the despot's fear!
Why stand ye in your coat of mail?
Why ye the Gates of Pride assail?—

"We stand, as courtiers nobly stand,
To guard the freedom of our land.
We stand—or fall! in this our might,
Defending what is true and right."

—Ye are a race of joy and song.
Wherefore your carols roll along?—
"We sing because our cause is just.
The God of nations is our trust.

We sing, for all our Princes swear
To laud our freedom, do and dare.
Our Kaiser stands, as firm as fate,
Against the vile oppressor's hate!

Our father's God we love, adore!
Who ruleth all the kingdoms o'er.
His wisdom strengthens our defence;
His sure hand holds the recompense!

Three cheers! grand Kaiser. Noble soul!
Aye, for thy Princes' wise control!
And cheers for thy brave Soldiery!
Who dare defy the enemy.

Nov. 1892.

The Vital Conflict.

The Victory of Truth.

The Battle Array.

Powers opposing Christ are doomed to fall!
Already o'er them hangs funereal pall.
The Prince of darkness must, in time, give way
To Him who made, and holds, the blessed day!

Malignant are the efforts seen along
The line of battle, midst the bustling throng.
Legions on legions come the subtle Foe,
To man the bloody fields of dying woe.
These forces are, indeed, austere and great;
Filled with the passion of a fearful hate.
Sabres and spurs are weltering in blood;
And, plunging still, augment the dismal flood
In malice vile they trample down the poor,
Piercing the cotter standing at his door.
Rebellion, red with anger, gloats the breast
Of him who murder looks upon with jest!

Faint are the cries of those who stem the tide
Of this fierce infamy, excess and pride—
Vain is all human hope, or human plan,
To overcome the enemy of man!

THE CHAMPION OF TRUTH.

But, there ariseth One! whose flowing locks
Betoken wrath which can withstand the shocks
Of fiery steel, with banners firm and gay,
To turn the battle tide the other way!
Whose feet of brass, whose mighty arm of strength,
Can lay the bold Goliath at full length;
Can swirl the vast commotion of this strife,
And bring foul Wrong to serve the King of Life;
Can chain the Leader of the rebel host,
By the great power of the Holy Ghost!
Will give him gall to drink, who glutted blood—
Impris'n 'mid walls of fire! which aye have stood
A warning in the universe of God,
To those who fail, thro' sin, to own his rod.

The Sceptic Corps.

First, in the band of traitors, come the horde
Of those who doubt the might of Jesus' sword.
The blatant Infidel, the Sceptic bold,
Who, while oppressed with hunger, heat or cold,
Denies the Force compelling him to bend
Before the powers which discomfort send
To his weak being; whose only redress
Is, all his need of mercy to confess,
As, food and clothing, water sweet and pure,
Like its Creator—grace forever sure.

But, infidelity of men can ne'er
Give to the world a solace for despair.
There are no benefits to poor mankind,
Which flow from this misanthropy so blind
No consolation for the aching head;
No hope for those who mingle with the dead.
Its trend, a dark and bottomless abyss,
Without a ray of hope, of joy, of bliss,
Or song, to cherish the expiring clod.
There is no heaven where there is no God!

Many a man has wearied of this strife;
Has bowed in prayer, and found the way of life;
Has from remorse escaped, to seek that rest
Found only on our Saviour's loving breast.
There laid his armor of rebellion by,
Learning, "'Tis blest to live—'tis gain to die."
The blood which flowed from our Redeemer's side
Remission gave, in Calvary's Crucified.

THE BIGOT'S BRIGADE.

Next comes the Bigot, clad in trim attire,
Tight-laced and proud, quite ready to expire;
Boasting of Truth, of which he hath the key;
And cries, "Now, if you want it, *come to me!*
Reproach for Christ his creed doth not receive.
He counts all "Holy days," and it would grieve
Him to the quick, if he did not keep all
The types and shadows, since poor Adam's fall.

He dates his school back to the start of time!
His Caps and Mantles, made from webs sublime,
Atone for each discrepancy of heart.
A dupe to all the tricks of lying art,

He counts his prayers upon a string of beads,
And, in devotions, all the fathers leads.
He prates about the "children of the world."
Against all "heresy" his darts are hurled,
In shape of "Bulls"—not having feet, nor head—
By which the innocent have oft been bled!

A tow'r of strength in things concerning self,
He, ever mindful of vain show and pelf,
Is struck with horror at the cry of shame;
For he, forsooth, hath all the right to blame!
"Infallibility!" In vain he tries
To bend the will of nations to his lies!
But, when they scoff at papal threatenings,
He woes of Tophet at their valor flings;
Kindling in wrath the Inquisitional Fire!
Testing the courage of the Martyr Sire!

Long were the polished Pharisees of old
Bewildered in this labyrinth so cold.
In vain they strove, by rites and formal show,
To find a solace for their heart-felt woe.
While texts of scripture decorate their gowns,

They look upon the godly poor with frowns.
Yet, think themselves the saviors of mankind,
Sent East and West, a proselyte to find.

A few, like Nicodemus, learned the way
Out of this dark abode, to light and day.
Jesus became the Star of all their hope.
They took his word to be faith's telescope.
And found in him true piety of heart,
Crying unto their woeful pride—"Depart!"
The finished work of Christ they there confess,
Renouncing all their own unrighteousness.
Thus, robed in his all-glorious attire,
They shine as clad in pentecostal fire.

THE DRUNKARD'S DIVISION.

And onward come, with frightful, horrid glare,
The Drunkard Makers' standards, high in air.
Inhuman bloats offset the gaudy train.
The Sot, the Harlequin, attempt in vain
To make the silly mob a pageant grand,
Or wake the plaudits of the incensed land!

For purposes of rapine are they wed,
That hearts and homes in terror may be bled!
To satisfy their raging thirst for spoil,
They rob the simple of rewarded toil.
Unnumbered agonies, shame and distress,
Come in their wake, to worry and oppress.
Serpents encircle all their weary path,
To make more keen the way to endless wrath!

To shield them in their bold assay of words,
The "Stars and Stripes" heralds the motly herds!
The Law they take to batter down all law,
To fill with gain their ever greedy maw.

But, soon the day will come, when Law shall be
Reversed, and made to strike, in action free,
Against the dictates of an angry mob,
In whose hot hearts malevolences throb
Athwart the weal of man, the force of truth,
The firm environment of age and youth.
The starry Flag shall carry in its fold
Some of the glory borne by it, of old;

When chains, once forged to gall the lowly slave,
Were broken by the One "mighty to save!"

THE FINAL ONSET.

The blood-stained banner of the Cross, unfurled,
Alone can bring to life a fallen world.
It represents unto the sons of men
That scene portrayed by the disciples' pen—
Love's desperation! when God gave his Son
From out his bosom, ere the race begun;
Who sprang into the field, with blood for blood,
And opened thence the soul-renewing flood!
Thro' strife to liberty he led his host,
Being anointed of the Holy Ghost.
Death only added terror to his foes!
For, breaking all his bands, from thence he rose
To press the battle tide more fiercely down,
As from his grasp he wrung the Victor's crown!

He "ever liveth" to renew the war—
Chains Sin and Satan to his battle car.
Kingdoms and thrones, opposing his career,

Are bro't to tremble 'neath his constant fear.
"Onward!"—the piercing cry, until his hand
Siezes the sceptre o'er all sea and land.
Then shall his praises evermore resound,
Wherever, clothed in white, the Saints are found;
'Till every hill and valley o'er the earth,
And roaring seas, shall chant Redemption's Birth!

1889.

www.ingramcontent.com/pod-product-compliance
Lightning Source LLC
Chambersburg PA
CBHW030908170426
43193CB00009BA/771